INDECENT HOURS

INDECENT HOURS

JAMES FUJINAMI MOORE

Four Way Books
Tribeca

Library of Congress Cataloging-in-Publication Data

Names: Moore, James Fujinami, 1989-
Title: Indecent hours / James Fujinami Moore.
Description: New York : Four Way Books, [2022]
Identifiers: LCCN 2021045633 | ISBN 9781954245129 (trade paperback) | ISBN 9781954245204 (epub)
Subjects: LCGFT: Poetry.
Classification: LCC PS3613.O56252 I53 2022 | DDC 813/.54--dc23
LC record available at https://lccn.loc.gov/2021045633

Four Way Books is a not-for-profit literary press. We are grateful for the assistance we receive from individual donors, public arts agencies, and private foundations including the NEA, NEA Cares, Literary Arts Emergency Fund, and the New York State Council on the Arts, a state agency.

We are a proud member of the Community of Literary Magazines and Presses.

Contents

for my mother,

who should not be held responsible

of the future, based on the flight patterns of certain birds

The forecast tells us rain. The bees
tell us no more. The newscaster tells us

all our best plastics are organic now.
The plastic tells us all our water

is safe to drink. The former
presidential candidate tells us

we must do our part
to fight the stereotype.

The man on the street
tells the stereotype to *take*

your fucking slant face
back to where it come.

The acid tells her skin acid.
The doctor tells her second-degree burns.

For a while, they told us to ration
our water because of drought.

Today, they tell us the rain
will stop maybe tomorrow,

or that the hills will collapse
& bury the houses in mud.

My father once told me
that after his home was buried

he ran away. When I was angry,
I told my parents

I'd run away, far away
and never ever

come back. Lit in the warm door-
light, the soft curve of my father

telling me *come back*. Americaness,
he tells me, is a temporary feeling

much like joy, or the flu.
In the rain, the archer

aims his arrow at the apple
atop his son's trembling head.

The archer tells me I am his son
before the arrow flies.

I am telling you, love,
I am not the archer, not his son,

not even the arrow
with its luxurious skirt, its

deadly full lips.
I am telling you

I am the sing of air between nock
& nock. I am telling you

in the leaving-sound, disrobing,
just before the stop.

1.

—And indeed the dead man gave no more trouble. Nothing at all happened.

notes on the fog

Dear brother,
after they brought him home,
to the home, all of us lost
weight.
It wasn't solidarity.
It was
decay. My shoulders eroded
from not hitting the gym.
I only write to you when the bad news comes.

You're tired. Do you want to go to bed? Do you want to just sit?

—

Dear brother,
how does the world make trenches,
if not out of dead fathers?

How does the world make fathers
if not out of driving to school?
(Did he read to you? He read to me too.)
He believed he raised a good son.
He raised a son

who didn't believe. And when he fell

he fell soundless

into the sea.

—

And so I use this detergent, and this setting should be fine?

Yes, but don't wash them with those clothes,
they're your father's, they're contaminated.

Okay, I'll
Put them on the floor.
The floor.
Not on top of the dryer,
the floor.

—

Dear brother,
they will bury him one plot over from you.

—

Dear brother,

this is what I wanted to say:

that the nurse came in
to do exercises with father, sets of curls,

flys, swims. It was a long-
term maintenance thing.

And mother stood up
all banana-yellow sanitary gown

and did them together, too,
and there was a move

the nurse called the Travolta,
and it looks just like you'd think, and our

mother (grave as a stone) bobs on her heels,
wiggles her hips, the nurse counts

the reps, and father is laughing and laughing

and lit in the eyes of the sun

and for a moment a moment
I'd never seen this (have you?)

they're dancing
          they're dancing again

—

Dear brother,

long parts of me are still wolves.

in the dormitories after dark

Understand:
they carried the boy
naked, hogtied to a pole,
down the hallway and I stood by.
It was punishment. He had
been late too many times,
and the older boys stripped
him down for—
amusement—he smiled
at first, too.
I stood there, beside—
or by—hearing them chant
shower, shower
their faces grabby at each
humiliation, shining
from inside with it & made
brighter & even then
I knew it was holy, a ritual to bind
us, a secret, the words
that even years later
lying beside you
I'd refuse to say. Lying by.
Even now, after your touch
has faded, I still remember this:

the great white mass of him
hung from the pole and swinging.
How after a while he stopped
smiling. How heavy it was
when it was my turn
to carry it.

the animals

It was probably meant to be
a lesson about responsibility—
how to care for something dependent
on you. In the kindergarten
we had hamsters,
mice, half a dozen fish;
an ark of approved animals
that we traded off daily
to feed. Each named
in crayon placard
placed before the cage. It was probably
meant to be a lesson about death—
a certain kind of death—
how later, one girl's grandpa died
and we were quiet, imagining
the size of the shoebox.
The day they were slaughtered,
skulls crushed, squished
in books, the fire
escape left cracked
open, the teacher wouldn't let us in.
Wouldn't tell us anything at all—
we milled outside, buzzed
with an ambient fear.

The officers who arrived
were kind. They humored
our awe, took fingerprints,
took us to a cell, took pity
and chipped in, they bought us
new hamsters, new mice,
each returned in cages
scrubbed clean.
It was probably
meant to be a lesson about order,
how safe we are in the law,
but by day's end it had become
about taking care,
of each other, really,
the tenderness lying in us all.

A week later it happened again.

American myth: the big chicken

Uncle Frank tells me to name all the Chinese myths I know.

. . . the five identical brothers?

The five identical brothers, Uncle Frank says, is a fake myth made by the white people who can't tell the slant-eyes apart.

Opium, Uncle Frank says, was a conspiracy to keep the Chinaman impotent so he would not breed.

Uncle Frank tells me that I am not Chinese and sometimes I agree.

Sometimes over dinner he would tell the scariest story I knew.

The story was called The Big Chicken and it featured a big chicken. *Bok bok.*

Uncle Frank was not a chicken, he was a dragon.

Tall as the trees, with a flattening voice.

At his first wedding ceremony, he wore a gorilla suit.

His first wife lit herself on fire.

Uncle Frank is a recluse now.

The Big Chicken gobbles up the street, *bok bok.*

The Big Chicken is behind you as you run, *bok bok.*

You hear it eating the door as you sprint upstairs, *bok bok.*

Outside the window the world is lightless like it was before creation and for a moment just a moment you're safe.

Then an enormous gleaming eye fills the window, so close to touch.

Bok bok.

midnight at Banshee

A dead boy walks into a bar
and orders a drink and the bartender says,
We don't serve your kind, dead boy

and the dead boy nods
his perforated head
and dead cold vodka pours out.

The bartender wipes it up.
A dead boy walks into
a bar and sits next to a dead boy

and says, *What's wrong with him?*
and the bartender says, *We don't*
serve dead boys

and the dead boy lays his slit
throat right down
and out pours a sweet ice-wine.

Like he's only asleep.
A dead boy walks into the bar
and says, *Whaddya got?* and the bartender says,

Two dead boys and a cocktail and the dead boy
smiles wide. His tongue unfolds
into a grey-furred moth, clicking.

His teeth go crackle-
crack! *I'll have what he's having*,
he grins, and his grin sloughs off its skin

and underneath is not a grin.

elegy for Third Engineer

For you, in the background of the movie,
riddled with bullets then spin-kicked
into glowing green goo

by Our Hero, Saint
Chiseled-Jaw who bursts in
at third act to save us all from

whatever. He's not my hero.
He killed you, Third Engineer,
along with Second and First

without so much as a one liner,
the ones he saves
for the named. You had

a name. Tenure track
at the Lair of Doom,
crushing on Dead

Secretary, waiting
to leave for the day.
Not even your death scream

was your own: it belonged to Man Bit
By Alligator, again. Third Engineer,
I would have lit candles

for you at the memorial service
because I've lit them before,
every time my people are killed

by a hero bursting through the door
and just hosing away.
He was glorious and terrible,

wasn't he, lit from below like the God
of School Lockdowns, God
of Hey What's That Noise God

of Ma'am I've Got
Some News About Your
Son god He

looks damn good, don't he?
So beautiful I could cheer.

upon closer examination, it is not a scarf

Only the liquid crystal screen
        separates us & I can
rewind the video
        so I do,
watch the man throw
        his eleven-month-old girl off the roof
over & over &
        over again. I saw it first streaming
over my Facebook,
        a blip descending scream
sandwiched between ten facts about
        anxiety that I probably won't believe
and an ad for the diapers
        I do not yet know I want, the
autoplays of Subarus
        & pain relief,
a reminder that gravity
        like fatherhood
is a neutral,
        irreversible force.
Scrubbing
        the video backwards
here is what
        I see: the baby

girl leaping up
        the lip of roof
to her daddy's open hands
        his soft hands undoing
over & over &
        over again
the weightless,
        ribboning noose.

the year in review

The man who will later
beat her shakes her

against the fence
wet in her winter coat.

He is screaming
a language I know. Tell me

something good
about the world.

Across the sea
there's a new rhythm

in bombs, the double tap:
meant to catch

those who try to help.
Some of what I know

sits in me like a pumpkin
gone to rot. Some days

defeat me as thoroughly
as a professional finger

breaker. I am all hands
waving, waving. Tell me something

good about this world
in a new tongue

that does not have
words like *cleansing*

or *scourge*.
Here I am, verbless, sighted.

Each word in my mouth
a bloodied, wrong stone.

2.

what I want to talk about is the awful propriety, the terrible morality, of the ant

25 apologies

I broke Robert Frost's
wheelbarrow. I lied, there
is meat in the soup. I
was drunk when I got
to that party. I forgot
that you were married
and didn't drink. I said I
was sorry when I wasn't
sorry. I wasn't as sorry
as I should have been.
In school I pushed you
down. In school I pushed
you down and liked it.
I broke Robert Frost's
wheelbarrow but in my
defense it was not a good
wheelbarrow. I can never
spell *receive*. I love you.
I loved you. I strayed. I
swallowed every twitched
desire and in my belly
they grew. I was *ooo*, I
was *ooo*, I was received. I
would eat your hollowed

throat if you'd let me,
your hollow salt lick
throat. I spilled lighter
fluid all over that stupid
goddamn wheelbarrow. I
saved all my best cruelties
for last. Each morning
I loved you. I loved you.
I was afraid. At night I
ate each vanishing star
with hunger, each corona
savaging my throat. I lied
to you. I couldn't fix it. I
let that wheelbarrow burn.

I don't always know what to do with this.

At the urinal, the man asks in his thick unplaceable accent if I know Bruce Lee.
Personally? No, we're not friends.
If you give a man an inch.
Shouting "Be like water! One inch punch! Kung fu kick!" as I walked away.
My soiled hands balled into fists.
I did not know what to do at the time.
A perfect ballet kick worthy of Bruce Lee?
I am not Bruce Lee, who was like water.
I did not kick him, flush the urinal with his grinning face, or deliver
   a stirring lecture on racist speech while gesticulating, dick in hand.
Afterwards, love, telling you I said *maybe this is a comment on my haircut.*
Maybe he doesn't know English that well.
Then I tried to understand.
If you gave Bruce Lee an inch, he could knock a man down.
Anyone.
I'm not saying I *know* the guy.
I am airless, I give away miles.
Maybe I am like Bruce Lee.
I form the shape of what I am given,
the way water does, splashing in a porcelain bowl,
splattering down with piss and chemical perfume,
that smell, that damp rot cherry.

to the white woman who asked if I was "one of those musical Asian children"

Let me answer by saying
    that the song used in the opening credits
        of the Green Hornet radio series

is Rimsky-Korsakov's "Flight
    of the Bumblebees," and if you know
        anything of classical music

you probably know this piece
    with its anxious sawing tremolos,
        growling sforzandos

that burst at the end the release almost
    of anxiety but then, then
        it isn't, let me say that

in the opera this is the song where
    the swan prince transforms to visit
        his father, transforms into the costume

of a bumblebee the way on the white comedian
    on late night TV tears off his suit to reveal
        a yellow and black-striped jumpsuit

underneath & he looks like
Bruce Lee, he says,
before he gets his ass kicked

and Bruce, I will always watch
a white comedian get his ass kicked
but goddamn, it's hard to look at you

and not hear your *HIIII-YAH!* yelps
in the mouths of bullies
every day after school

when I'd pretend
to be the loyal sidekick,
like Kato, saving

the white master
from his mistakes
let me tell you that

that no, I had no sleeping gas,
no gadgets of mercy, I was awake
to see him transform

back out

the back of that

forbidden yellow thing.

August in Vermont

My body is sweet to the blood-zip.
They hover, waiters in the eaves.
I am ample feast.
There is something erotic about the itch, isn't there?
Something sexy about the plague.
A stranger with his long-hooked mask.
Don't you just love a good proboscis?
Juniper berry, carnation, a vinegar sponge.
If eradicated, an expert says the entire biome would not suffer the
    lack of the mosquito.
To avert sickness, Grandfather says
avoid the bad apples.
What is the quality of a bad apple?
The memory of a better fruit?
I am a better fruit to the blood-zip than J.
How I pity him his unbothered skin.
Each bite a map on my body, each a small town of itch.
Nails be the homecoming hero, moon-kissed with blood.
The mosquito carries with it several diseases which taken together kill a
    significant portion of humankind.
Their bellies swollen with chills, ache.
The bodies in their plague-pits, each on each.

notes from a digging machine (imagine a worm) tunneling through the center of the earth

Weeks from the face
of trees, we fill
our mouths with earth.
Dirt has a taste,
the geologists say: light
puffs of sediment,
the rich chocolate
clay. A sailor
spits diamonds
from his teeth.
For three days straight
we burrow through coal.
The Captain says
it purifies our bodies.
The Captain says
we will find old
Atlantis, lost Mu,
our mythic homelands, China—
Cheers at every
impossible place. Each mouth
a wide black tunnel,
each belly layered, pregnant
with the only history
of where we come from.

❧

The hours mock us
absent a sun.
We hold fast
our routines:
swabbing, eating,
staring blankly
out the useless
portholes.
Our sweaty bunk-gasps
band each day.
Still we drift.
A month since we left?
A year? The ship moans
under the pressure.
We count our breaths'
drip down the walls.
Longing marks its own calendar
along the hem.
Perhaps we left yesterday,
we said yesterday.
Almost certainly
yesterday.

❧

Yesterday
a forest of mushroom trees.
Mycelium, finger-thick,
pulsing with light.
We see in their branching fruit
prophecy, neurology,
maps of our own brains.
My first kiss sprouts from a bearded
tooth. My first steps birth
networks of death caps.
Our regrets, our kinks,
our gilled, dry shame. The first mate chokes
in the pale shiitake light.
Love beckons. One man (he is young)
breaks apart the caps & fills
his mouth as his lover
looks gently on, his hands reaching
through their torsos, hands
reaching up through the loamy floor.
We are envious of their tongues of light,
of how their mouths arrive.
The captain says *time to go*.

❧

We are so close.
Gravity straps us to our beds.
The air lies heavy in unsummer.
The boatswain's whip
croons on his neck.
Tomorrow whispers
the captain out the bedsores
of his bed. The engines—
how long since they've been fed?
Me, I've handfast
to the cool, the perforated
steel stair. *Tomorrow*
says the captain. We still cannot rise.
Blind we move forward, tunneling
through the heated dark.
Imagine a worm, love,
as it flees the knowing sun.
Tomorrow.
certainly

tomorrow

notes on an illegal face cream

My lover puts snail slime on her face
each evening before bed.

It moisturizes, she says. *If I moisturize*
I will live forever—

So far, no evidence
of eye stalks.

The beauty product is Korean. My lover
is beautiful to me. In evenings

the street lights inscribe mazes in her skin.
A snail can survive

just about anywhere
curious boys are not:

abandoned gardens, the abyss
of the sea. Left alone

some live for a decade or more.
Why do my hands

ache with cruelty?
Standing in my garden

with salt in hand,
watching each face dissolve away,

each popping in quiet,
ruined applause.

still life w/ shirt

Describe it.

My oldest shirt is a men's collared shirt by Oscar de la Renta, white stripes on white. French cuffs, single breast pocket. I don't know the size, or the year.

Describe its history.

My grandfather wears it to go work every day at Bank of America, first in Yokohama, and then in LA. After his retirement, his wife hangs it up.

Describe it blind.

Ribbed of fabric. Stored sleep scent. Fraying towards the neck and waist, like ants. Tiny, creeping pills.

Describe how it fits.

The shoulders and collars are perfect.
The sleeves are too short.

Describe in color.

White of yellow. Old cream. In direct sunlight, stained. Over skin, white of skin. Ivory of a dead animal shot with silver. New bone.

Describe how it fits.

At my graduation, my grandfather with his hiss & spray of breath. At his grave, it doesn't itch.

Describe it.

For months, he trained to walk down the aisle.
On a treadmill, blowing up balloons.

Describe it on him.

Describe it.

Walk like you have three men walking behind you.

Describe it.

Each wearing, some part

notes on the phrase shikata ga nai, written after a Colorado state representative says in 2017 that the internment camps were justified because "in the heat of battle there isn't time to distinguish who is a citizen and who is not," or: it cannot be helped.

I am so tired of talking about Manzanar.
Lord, let me talk about anything
else instead. The moon, the sea, even fucking flowers
I'd rather write than these desert stories muled as a kid,
old as black bile, a myth, America,
of your forgiveness, of what couldn't be helped.

That phrase in rōmaji, *it cannot be helped*
engraved on stones they sell at the gift shops in Manzanar
alongside baseballs, tiddlywinks, tin American
planes with their tin tiny bombs, anything
a souvenir, a replica poster for the kids
saying where to go, hiding behind the "Japanese-style" flower

vase on sale. Some days I say history and mean ikebana.
Sometimes bonsai. Question: With sharp enough clippers, can you help
any tree grow small? With sharp enough clippers, can you outlive your kids?
A tree is a reflection. In the bark, ōoji's unendurable face. Before Manzanar,
there were strawberries. After, there were also strawberries. Anything
can be celebrated with strawberries in America,

your fields promising red on your lips, your teeth. America,
I still whisper this poem. In your heart even the sakura
blooms for your old dead soldiers, everything

pink, everything brief. The Paiute lived here before Manzanar,
were removed,   and returned,   and helped
build too. You conscripted our dying to dig our graves. Each boy

giving their mute answer to the guards, each boy
saying *yes*   saying   *no*   *no.* Our traitors
fought for you, America. They just wanted to go home.
Where I'm from there's no cherry trees, just dead wisteria
washed in drought. At Manzanar
I was a garden, I was a maid, I sold groceries, bled rabbits, all

blooms with a spade. I was your issei, your nisei, your sansei
I was your viper-hatched son.
Question: *Hast thou gods before me? When have you prayed?*
According to your survey, my Americanness is irrational.
They say you planted victory gardens
in our absence. They say you'll let us return.

Great-uncle says the suffering helped, America.
He gave his kids his citizen pride. Today only flowers
bloom over his grave. He went blind too, after Manzanar.

notes on the return

after m. washington

back / to go
back / to go back to the place
you have come from / to the
place you have come from return
/ to return / return as a swallow
might / a swallow might fly
as young as eighteen days /
eighteen days out from our
journey here you had a camera
/ a camra / a cmra in my hand i
am recording / i am recording
a man he is being arrested /
being arrested he has no hands
but he screams / he screams get
back / get back to where you
have come from / where you
have come from there are more
trees / trees holding their nests
/ nests above the sidewalk /
the sidewalk my front door /
my front door once we found a
fledgling that had fallen / fallen
or been pushed / pushed out
the door my lover held it in her

hands she lined a shoebox with
soft she brought it limping to
the shelter / to the shelter but it
died / it died across the island
six miles as the swallow flies /
the swallow flies two hundred
miles on a clear good day / on a
clear good day someone says to
return / to return to the place
you have come from / the place
you have come from a beat fast
and dying / dying between two
cupped hands

I want to tell you about even the fucking flowers.

How it is too much.
The wisteria spilling
off the arbors. The bees
weave their industry
through the bells.
It rained here
off and on
for hours, or years,
and now, briefly, stopped.
Each bustle of flowers
abundant, rustling,
streaked with tears.
Have you ever smelled
the wisteria, M?
It is so faint
I bury my nose
into their dozens
before I hear my name,
each scent curled
in fists of lilac
lapping at my face.
For weeks they hang
in their beauty,
and then sing again,

sing out their thorns
beneath my bare feet.
M, spilled over the ground
a raceme of wisteria smells
the same in rot. Now I am here
at the ends of myself.

3.

all that you have been imagining was an illusion—except the calling of the dead

Salem, Oregon

For a long time, I thought they burned witches
in Oregon. East Coasters find this hilarious.
They say there is something irrevocably New England
about it: black gowns in the city square, flames
& autumn leaves. But I am a Californian, and the old terror
of fire is my blood. They burned no witches
in Salem, they were crushed or hanged.
A good hanging (did you know?) is mostly math: a drop-
length proper, a knot hugging the ear.
These days witches make pilgrimages to Salem,
where they sell tchotchkes of the dead
to the young. These days my Tinder says find Hot Witches
Near You. It promises with just one simple quiz
I can discover my Patronus, my secret talent,
every animal of my past
guilty lives. Salem,
forgive my jelly eyes, my dumb
big hooves, my trespasses.
How good I was
at staying in my place.

tetra

The fish was immortal,
I think. It was the first pet
I ever asked for & received,
a tiny shiver of orange
that I fed flakes to
every day until I got
tired. You were beautiful
& still are. Did you know
that a tetra will eat another
given the absence of food? I tried to kill
the fish. I poured soap
in the tank, dripped in
bleach, strangled it for a minute
in air before returning it to where
it swam cheerfully on. Nothing
worked but the kitchen knife
and the toilet, where it left
a spooling blood-ribbon
that I flushed over and over
to disappear. I never told you
how you began to smell
of hot steel, of rust. The brittle
way you'd wake lie there.
My carrion. My carry-over

love. Let me bring you home
in a clear plastic bag, won
from the fair. I'll never
get tired of it.

in 1984, a lake with swan boats

It's around then they
contemplate buying a hot dog stand
in the park—by the lake—
where now I'm not sure I've ever seen
a stand, just the little iron taco carts
and abuelas hawking swaddled
tamales from Styrofoam chests.
It's midwinter. Gloria Molina
had been elected to city council
and workers dig into the lake-bank's
silt, replanting the lotus for summer.
Every night my parents talk,
ever since the election
that my father lost
they talk of
hot dog stands. A stable living.
The conversation circling
the darkened rooms
at a scavenger pace.
Hot dogs & the election's loss,
their firstborn's dead—
so, for that matter,
are the lotus in the lake,
that will last all of two years

before they too wither overnight.
Every night, my mother rows over
the mirror water and pulls
the new plants out to eat,
the perforated roots that grant
foresight or, maybe,
forgetfulness. We did everything
to wake him, she says,
but he didn't move.
Hence, the hot dogs.
She wears shawls
in summer. Father joins a cult.
There are hairshirts
and new brittle smiles.
Together my parents stain lamb's blood
on their clothes, on the bedsheets,
on everywhere but the front door.

poem ft. Los Angeles

after Dean Rader

The joke is that
there are no angels in Los Angeles.

Like the pickup line: *hey girl, did you fall*
from heaven or come from Los Angeles?

Trick question—everyone knows no one
comes from Los Angeles.

But let me tell you there is something
to the light in Los Angeles.

Unflattering, unrepentant, a light for shooting,
to shoot. No, Los Angeles

is no different than your hometown, really,
it has Target, it's a trap. I'm from Los Angeles,

and let me tell you I have seen angels,
let me tell you they had rubbernecker eyes, in Los Angeles

they have celiac's and burn storefronts
and smoke. Yes, they still smoke in Los Angeles.

My father, his father, me. Yes, they quit,
they died. In Los Angeles

there's neighborhoods between *dead*
and *not doing that anymore*, in Los Angeles

I'm not drunk, I'm on brand.
There's no smog in Los Angeles,

just those spectacular coughs of sunset. My father said
you live seven years in Los Angeles

you'll never really leave. Which sounds like Persephone,
or maybe bullshit. Here's a joke, Los Angeles,

to hold in your heart of stop-and-go:
dear Los Angeles,

it's all twenty minutes away
from here

to the woman reading erotic prayers on the bus this morning

may god swallow
you may she
not chew may
the journey be long
down the esophagus'
soft flex may you rest
on each spine pin
making circles
a toothpick between god's lips *O*
to be an eel nailed
to the cook's slat-board,
built of tweezered
delicate bone may she
save you like all the gods
of my childhood
babes borne out peach pits men
who called birds women dragging
ropes from themselves
like sailors pulling anchors
from their skins, may you be
forgiven the way the lakewater
killed all the lotus
over & over &
no planting we could do

until one summer they thrived, gently slapping
their great wings against the shore &
were stolen the next year.

tendering

It is the stubble
I love first

with an envy.

A ridge of scrub runs
along this canyon edge.

I hate hiking.

True story:
Near our home there was a garden.

To get there:
hike the canyon edge.

In the garden there is a stone
bench in shade,
faucets of cool water,
dog-bowls to drink.

(A bead of sweat
buries its face into his scruff.)

For God's sake *Yes*
this is a memory of thirst.

The way saying *parched*
blows over the drying tongue.

In this moment we are both relentlessly alive.

(Brother, in the garden they said there was a tree for you.)

There is a map in his lips.

I hate hiking, but obviously let's explore.

For God's sake *okay*
I'll skip the explicit—

Time drifts apart.

On Facebook, he writes that his little brother died.

Suicide, he says.

True story:
Near our home there was a forest.

Once, and then a fire.

(brother, do you remember this?)

(brother, it was around when you died.)

For God's sake

I'm sorry, I've written again
something
something something
~~something~~ something
something about a tree.

Too thin
for a boy
to climb.

For God's sake
we water that tree
anyway.

It is loved so loved.

and dead,

but still.

third date

In the indecent hour
let me hang up my shame.

Let me tell you of softness
and of hardness and of

promises. I promise you this:
                                        filth

past our first taste of awkward—
the negotiation of *oh like*

this? what if
            mmm—

fumbles of zippers,
buttons, lace, a shirt's
                    soft sigh

open. the goosebump breeze.
an invitation   first
to what is tender,
then what is rough, then to your tongue
of tarried vowels, each syllable the breath's

long linger: *acacia.*   *qualia.*
                  evacuee.

I'll whisper *ululate*
between your thighs.

Let's play for tops
and bottoms. The body's
wet slap. Scream
your tally scratches,
my consonant mess.
Name me Monster. Name me Daddy.
Name me Stranger,
Murderer, Miss.
Let's cross state lines together
with someone else's blood
in your lap. Let's make my mouth
your laundry.
My hands
the hangman's
deft rope. Say yes,
love, to the drop.
                We're done decency.
Come lay down with me

in the kennel, amidst the dogs,
abandoned to hunger. Come
eat
eat &

eat,

each one of your grins
etching into my bones.

notes after sex

The butler in my mouth
has a funny name, like Evelyn

or Applebee, and is of the old
school, as they say, wears tails

and waits up nights, frowns
at the incorrigible company

I keep. The whole house
smells of damn curry spice, he shouts,

and your cheeks are peeling
their wallpaper again. The butler

in my mouth does not get along
with the maids of my throat.

He does not understand the frilly
fetish uniforms, why they titter

and never dust. Bless him. He
has work aplenty, wrestling

unexpected houseguests to the floor.
My god, the Russian girl

again? Yes, good Cornwallis, we live
in sin and it is our only comfort.

Be a dear and break out the good
bourbon. The war is not yet come.

letters from Japan

Tokyo, 10.10.18

3 AM, my old drummer heart.
The red distant
semaphore is pins over
skin. I know that not everything
is a code, M, but it feels that way
in this quiet. If I believed in stars
I could tell you that the palace's pattern
of window-lights means chrysanthemum,
that far below the old emperor sleeps
while tourists snap selfies
in his immaculate
moat. I live in this hotel instead.
Naked, yet not cold. Every new
surface giving me back in borrowed light.

Tokyo, 12.10.18

On the street,
nobody touches.
I could spend
an hour watching
this child fish
autumn's dead
leaves from this
square pool. The gin
is waking me up.
Today I visited
the statue galleries:
nests of tangled
legs, vulva, crooked
knee. In one, the Buddha
emerges, blinking, from
an armpit. You would love
it here, M. The platform's suicide gates
are a soothing blue.

Kyoto, 15.10.18

At Sanjūsangen-dō, I search
the thousand faces of Kannon
for one that looks like you.
As if I could even
recognize myself
serene, clad in gold. Today
like every day I am trying
to be a man so I imagine
shooting arrow after arrow
down the length of the hall
until my fingers are stripped down
to bone. Every face
has a halo around it
like a migraine, or a bullseye. Read
the signs: Carve dreams
into wax candles. Pray.
Touch the statues
you are permitted to touch
with their patina of oil and skin
given so even the blind
can see the god's face.

Kyoto, 16.10.18

The giant invisible Buddha
lives in a silo behind the main temple
that, after a bribe, the priest takes us to see.
He tells us proudly that it is larger
than the Buddha in Ibaraki, which is
only 120 meters tall,
made only of stone. Here,
the Buddha is a set of footprints
            and a column of air
                        and chanting before the altar
                                    and he is 150, 200, 1000 meters tall....

Before we leave, we feed the Buddha
our handfuls of plastic lotus leaves.
There are no guidelines to wish
so I think of you. Each bright
prayer falling through
the blessed body of air, to kiss
his massive feet lined in silver,
embedded into the marble
whole afterlives away.

in this instance I am inflicted with vulnerability, which is a curse

I have no soul at all,
eaten alive
by ants filigreed
with skulls. I am shot
full of poison. Once,
my doppelganger
runs me through,
cackling.

I wake to begin again.

God,

I wish I was immune
to goddamn poison.

song

There is a songbird
that opens every morning
with five notes perfectly
syncopated: low high
mid, mid, mid. Across

five states and twenty
years, singing out the mouth
of the deep city or the backcountry's
lonely quiet. Five notes,
unanswered,

clear. Once, I watched
my friend whistle birdcalls at the trees
and heard them call
back. I've never seen
the morning's songbird—it could be,

for all I know, an owl—
and some mornings it mocks
with solitude and
empties my bed and I stand
at the window in my underwear,

tracking the branches
with a BB gun. Other mornings
it's as much a lullaby
as the sirens of my childhood,
those helicopter blades

I still hear foolishly
as angel wings. If I were a nun
I'd be the kind that hides chocolate
under her bed, my habit rustled
with the wrappings. Some mornings

the bird sings and I whistle back, and he says
nothing. After twenty years
I suspect he has learned
to be alone with his five
perfect notes

a song for only one other,
who must be beautiful—
why else would he
wait this long?

in El Niño
after Christopher Kempf

We froze water bottles
& sucked

the long fingers of ice out
the necks. We bought hand

-held fans with built-in water
sprays and hoped the batteries

wouldn't bleed.
We wore light up sneakers.

The sneakers split
on the asphalt heat.

Their mouths yawning,
whispering each

to each in dying
Morse code. People died

in El Niño. We told stories
of babies in cars & abuelas

without AC & that one kid
who fell asleep & burned

and burned. We were four
in El Niño he coulda

been me. There was only one god
in El Niño & it was El Niño & we sacrificed

our virgins & bought sunshades
for our cars. We were all virgins

before El Niño. We yelled
at the weatherman

who said the El Niño, his redundant
the El Niño.

His coffin-tanned face smiling, promising
it'd never be this hot again.

American myth: The Three Identical Grandfathers

My grandfather, who is white
tells me stories of the Pacific Theatre.
The jungles, the sweat-on-skin,
the insects fat and lazy with blood.
He tells me of the time his unit tried to save our boys,
but The Enemy locked them in a bunker,
poured in gasoline, and lit them on fire instead.
The smell, he says, *the smell*,
his face turned away in memory, maybe,
or just to avoid looking at mine.

*

My uncle, who is Chinese
tells me I am not Chinese
if I do not know the Chinese myths.
Here is the most important one, he says:
one day they came from over the sea
& they burned the world down.

*

A brief historical fact: after he failed
to commit suicide, after he was captured,

on trial for his atrocities after the war,
Tōjō Hideki requested a set of teeth.
Just the upper set. To speak clearly at trial.
The dentist, who was white, made him a new set
with the words
REMEMBER PEARL HARBOR
drilled in code behind the veneers.
A prank, he said.
Funny as hell, his supervisor said.
Three months later, they ground off the code.

*

My grandfather, who is Japanese, had
harmless, trembling hands.
In an interview, his quiet voice comes back
through the crackled tape, long after his death.
What did you do during the war, grandpa?
I was kamikaze. And then I was funeral corps.
I covered bodies in quicklime, in caves, in the hills.
I remember worms. the smell.

*

My grandfather, who is Chinese,
died right after the war.
A botched operation, or so the story goes.
The same operation that lives in the belly
of my lover, beneath the silver scar I trace
at night sometimes. If we have children,
they will sleep beneath it too,
kicking their wordless,
hammered code.

*

A myth: my great grandmother, who is Chinese
stands on a bridge somewhere in the Ming province.
It is a hundred years ago.
It is yesterday, and she is beautiful.
In the distance, the drone of a far-off plane.
So far off, it could be anyone's.
She hides her eyes behind her hand.
The missile hides its face behind the sun.
There is a kind of light that burns
and grows—*O it is beautiful, do*
you see? The burning

that writes the histories
to come.

4.

afterward he often tried to listen to the conversation of ants

American myth: Kim v. Mancini

They say if you die outside the home
your spirit wanders forever.
Summer is the season
of ghosts: each black-hat stranger
hiding his pale face. Surround
yourself with oranges,
pierce your skull
with silver pins.
What is this endless weeping?
To wander forever
is a terrible fate.

Boom Boom's father was a boxer too.
Shrapnel from the war living under his skin.

Let me tell you the story the way I remember it : On November 13th, 1982, the contender Kim Duk-Koo stepped into a ring outside Caesars Palace to fight the lightweight champion Ray Boom Boom Mancini. Kim was a brawler, by which I mean he liked to get close. Mancini was too. Most boxing newsmen favored Ray, friend of Frank Sinatra, friend of Stallone, real-life Rocky Balboa, the last Great White Hope. Forgive them. They did not know what was to come. The fight no one could forget burns holes through history. For thirteen rounds, Ray and Kim go toe-to-toe: each round Mancini storms out, each round Kim returns. Their feet touch. Kim tears open Mancini's left ear, puffs his left eye, takes a looping hook on his head that swells Boom Boom's hand to twice its normal size. In the eleventh Ray buckles Kim's knees. I want you to imagine this because it is important. The crowd rising to cheer the Korean as he comes to his feet. See him, slick as a newborn in sweat and blood. The announcer's voice booms like a hungry God : "THIS IS THE CHALLENGER DUK-KOO KIM. YOU MAY NOT HAVE HEARD OF HIM BEFORE. YOU WILL REMEMBER HIM TODAY." Forgive me. This is not the story the way you want to remember. In the fourteenth, a right missed left right. Duk-Koo head snaps back. For a brief moment he flies, is weightless, free. Crashes down. Pulls himself up on the ropes, staggers. Falls back into the ref's arms. The match is called. Under his skull, already the blood's early bloom. It takes four days for him to die, his mother by his side. Three months later she drinks pesticide. Five months later the ref commits suicide. That same month Kim's son is born. "There's no joy in it now, no proudness," says Boom Boom, years later. In his hotel room before the match, Kim writes the words *live or die* on the bedside lampshade. The words painting the walls as he sleeps.

Dear brother,

I never watched the fight.
These days it's all on YouTube.
In the thumbnail,
an old man in a red jacket
frowns & frowns.
Is he the ref? Boom Boom's father
of the shrapnel heart?
A spectator
like me?

Someone comments *a benchmark—*
it's sad
someone had to—

Brother, it has not made me smarter.
Not tougher. Just slower in how I die.

I knew him better than his mother, said Ray.

There isn't much record I can find
of Mrs. Kim except that she was poor.
A peddler of bean curd. That she fled
an abusive man, a man of great rage.
That sometimes her son was so hungry
she begged in the street. She raised
a fighting man, but don't read so much
into that—so did mine. What did she say
the first time he came home bruised,
bleeding? My mother asked when
I was planning to stop. I wasn't
planning to stop. They sit
at tea. Mrs. Kim in death's
white obi, my mother in her black
living crepe. I do not think
they would talk. Just sit in their
enormous, dead-son silence.
You never get over
losing a child,
my mother said once
unexpectedly. Far above,
the ring-lights shattering out.

Tell me, outsider, how you remember it. On November 13th, 1982, the contender Kim Duk-Koo beautiful, his bruise-boy face stepped into a ring outside he said we could go if he won to Caesars Palace to fight fight fight the lightweight champion Ray Boom Boom of his fists, his terrible fists Mancini. Kim was a brawler a warrior by which I mean he liked to get close, too close stay away. Mancini was too. Stay away. Most boxing newsmen favored Ray not my Kim, friend of Frank Sinatra his voice on the radio, we danced to his songs, friend of Stallone I do not know him, real-life Rocky Balboa I couldn't bear to watch, the last Great White Hope. Forgive them. Why? They did not know what was to come. The fight no one could try harder to forget burns holes through history. For thirteen rounds, Ray and Kim go toe-to-toe: each round Mancini storms out, each round Kim returns. Like lovers, like he loved me. Their feet touch. His child inside me. Kim tears open Mancini's left ear oh yes, puffs his left eye yes yes, takes a looping hook on his head that swells Boom Boom's hand to twice its normal size. In the eleventh Ray buckles Kim's knees. no. I want you to imagine this because it is important. How many times I have imagined it. The crowd rising to cheer the Korean as he comes to his feet. See him, slick as a newborn in sweat and blood. He was my baby. His baby was mine. The announcer's voice booms like a hungry God into the land of Moriah:

"THIS IS THE CHALLENER DUK-KOO KIM WHOM THOU LOVEST. YOU MAY NOT HAVE THE FIRE, THE WOOD, THE LAMB FOR THE BURNT OFFERING, ABRAHAM. WE WILL COME BACK FOR YOU." Forgive me God will provide. This is the place which God had told him of. This is the story the day the sky fell down.

I have buried the memory of all that
insurmountable grief and shame the
most common problems for a boxer it's
bound to be that way He was smiling
good looking That'll take your heart away
cheekbone fractured cranial nerve ribs
broken half a dozen teeth knocked out
the bell no one hears it painfully, he tries
to pull himself to lurching I have buried
Heroes where's the bell coal-heavers,
watermen, and butchers' boys eating away
with both hands Why doesn't the
referee stop it? Why?
                                        it's bound to be that
way long after his death a panorama of
low, dirty, happy, brutal, sentimental
courage, nothing but magnificent courage
he is fighting with This is no fight There's
only one way he was still an innocent
There's only one way I think it was not
your fault Without boxing Everything
was lost There's only one way for a
champion to finish Born in the torrid
heat From one mother to another I want
you to live with us I have the memory He
was big and good looking and smiling
when he came into the ring he is your
son I am his son I think it is was not your
fault You deserve

On November 13th, 1982,
the contender Kim Duk-Koo stepped into a ring outside Caesars Palace
to fight the lightweight champion Ray Boom Boom Mancini.

imagine
The crowd rising to cheer

all that I couldn't make beautiful

The summer I turned ten
 I took a job making
medallions of the Virgin
 of Guadalupe to be cast
into gold-leafed bronze
 that first was traced
in green wax I'd paint
 into each edge,
her wimpled head,
 the soft folds
of her cloak, every place
 a bubble might stick
but I wasn't good at it
 not at all
& peeling each out
 their rubber molds
I'd find holes out
 her mouth, her feet
of roses, that summer
 I wanted the accompanist
but I didn't know how—
 do you understand?—
I did not know how
 I wanted her

there was a gap
between my mouth &
my mouth—
at the factory nailed
to the wall the sculpture
of a woman nude, legs
spread & one morning
my boss ran his rough
clay fingers up & down
& up her thighs, flicking
her plaster clit, laughing
the rollercoaster
of your life
that summer I did not
kiss the accompanist I made golems
out the stolen scraps
of clay I plunged
my hand into the vat
of wax I wanted
so badly to be clean
each face of the Virgin
blameless, and serene,
a flaw in every one.

notes

The interstitials on pages 7, 27, 51, and 85 are taken from Lafcadio Hearn's *Kwaidan: Stories and Studies of Strange Things*, originally published in 1904.

"American myth: the big chicken" references the book *The Five Chinese Brothers*, an American children's book written by Claire Huchet Bishop and illustrated by Kurt Wiese, and originally published in 1938 by Coward-McCann.

"elegy for Third Engineer" references the Wilhelm Scream, a stock film sound effect that has been used since 1951. The recording was originally titled "Man getting bit by an alligator, and he screamed."

"upon closer examination, it is not a scarf" is based on an incident in 2017, in which a man livestreamed a murder-suicide on Facebook Live.

"25 apologies" references an incident in which the speaker Robert Frost burns Robert Frost's wheelbarrow. I didn't do that. The wheelbarrow is fine.

"still life w/ shirt" quotes Oscar de la Renta. The original line was a suggestion to runway models: "Walk like you have three men behind you."

"notes on the phrase shikata ga nai . . ." references the most famous of the Japanese internment camps of WWII, Manzanar. In addition, some lines reference a series of loyalty questionnaires that were issued to the interned Americans, the most famous of which was used to judge their "Americanness" through a series of statements and questions. This survey culminated in two final questions certifying that those in the camps would be "willing to serve in the armed forces of the United States on combat duty, wherever ordered," and would additionally "swear unqualified allegiances to the United States of America and faithfully defend the United States from any or all attack by foreign or domestic forces, and forswear any form of allegiance or obedience to the Japanese emperor, or other foreign government, power or organization." Some of those who answered yes to both questions became the 442nd Infantry Regiment, the most decorated unit in American History. Those who refused upon the principal that the question implied the legitimacy of their internment became known as the No-No Boys, and were considered "disloyal" and sent to the internment camp at Tule Lake.

"poem ft. Los Angeles" takes its form from a poem by Dean Rader, "Cartography; or American Allegory I," from his book *Self-Portrait as a Wikipedia Entry* (Copper Canyon Press, 2017).

"in El Niño" takes its form from a poem by Christopher Kempf, "In The 90s," from his book *Late in the Empire of Men* (Four Way Books, 2017).

"13 rounds for Kim v. Mancini": Much of the history for this piece has been sourced from various articles, most prominently "A Step Back: Families Continue to Heal 30 Years After Title Fight Between Ray Mancini and Duk-koo Kim" by Mark Kriegel, as well as his book *The Good Son : The Life of Ray "Boom Boom" Mancini* (Simon & Schuster,

2012). In particular, p. (*63 in current order)* is composed entirely of quotes from that book, from the book *The Sweet Science* by A. J. Liebling (North Point Press, 1951) as well as transcriptions from two YouTube videos: "Jack Dempsey and Jess Willard—The Worst Beating in Boxing History —W/ Commentary" & "USA Boxing Physicians Guide."

As a final note: in July of 2010, the son & girlfriend of Kim Duk-Koo, Jiwan & Young-Mi, met Ray Mancini for the first time since the 1982 fight. They had dinner, drank wine from Mancini's winery Southpaw, and met his three children, Nina, Leonard, and Ray-Ray. During the dinner, Ray said "I felt guilty about what happened for a long time. I felt guilty because of your mother. I felt guilty that you never met your father." In response, Jiwan said to Ray, "I think it is not your fault. You deserve. Maybe now your family will be more happy."

acknowledgments:

Some of these poems have appeared in previous form in the following publications: AAWW's *The Margins,* Barrow Street's *4x2, The Brooklyn Rail, Guesthouse, The Pacifica Literary Review*, and *Prelude.*

So much goes into a book, and so much is owed. I am deeply, deeply grateful.

For the folks at Four Way Books: for Ryan Murphy's keen, dry eye, for Clarissa Long's post-it-notes and comforting winks. For Hannah Matheson's exclamations that saved many a line and sharpened many more. For Bridget Bell's perfect pitch & precise queries.

For Martha Rhodes, whose steady faith saw this book, and me, through. For my teachers, Catherine Barnett, Anselm Berrigan, Karin Gottshall, Yona Harvey, Donna Masini, Tom Sleigh, Mary Szybist, Emily Jungmin Yoon, and so many more, who encouraged me to reach further than I thought I could.

For my friends who showed me how to read my own work, how to take it more seriously, and myself less.

For the Bread Loaf Waiters in 2018, last & best.

SH, for lighting the way through.

MW, for reading me first.

For my father. For my brother.

And for Leah, for always, and a little bit more.

Thank you for your kind attention.

James Fujinami Moore's work has appeared or is forthcoming in Barrow Street's *4x2*, *The Brooklyn Rail*, *Guesthouse*, AAWW's *The Margins*, the *Pacifica Literary Review*, and *Prelude*. He has received support from Poets House, Bread Loaf, and the Frost Place, and received his MFA from Hunter College. He lives in Los Angeles. This is his debut collection.

Publication of this book was made possible by grants and donations. We are also grateful to those individuals who participated in our 2021 Build a Book Program. They are:

Anonymous (16), Maggie Anderson, Susan Kay Anderson, Kristina Andersson, Kate Angus, Kathy Aponick, Sarah Audsley, Jean Ball, Sally Ball, Clayre Benzadón, Greg Blaine, Laurel Blossom, Adam Bohannon, Betsy Bonner, Lee Briccetti, Joan Bright, Jane Martha Brox, Susan Buttenwieser, Anthony Cappo, Carla and Steven Carlson, Paul and Brandy Carlson, Renee Carlson, Alice Christian, Karen Rhodes Clarke, Mari Coates, Jane Cooper, Ellen Cosgrove, Peter Coyote, Robin Davidson, Kwame Dawes, Michael Anna de Armas, Brian Komei Dempster, Renko and Stuart Dempster, Matthew DeNichilo, Rosalynde Vas Dias, Kent Dixon, Patrick Donnelly, Lynn Emanuel, Blas Falconer, Elliot Figman, Jennifer Franklin, Helen Fremont and Donna Thagard, Gabriel Fried, John Gallaher, Reginald Gibbons, Jason Gifford, Jean and Jay Glassman, Dorothy Tapper Goldman, Sarah Gorham and Jeffrey Skinner, Lauri Grossman, Julia Guez, Sarah Gund, Naomi Guttman and Jonathan Mead, Kimiko Hahn, Mary Stewart Hammond, Beth Harrison, Jeffrey Harrison, Melanie S. Hatter, Tom Healy and Fred Hochberg, K.T. Herr, Karen Hildebrand, Joel Hinman, Deming Holleran, Lillian Howan, Thomas and Autumn Howard, Catherine Hoyser, Elizabeth Jackson, Jessica Jacobs and Nickole Brown, Christopher Johanson, Jen Just, Maeve Kinkead, Alexandra Knox, Lindsay and John Landes, Suzanne Langlois, Laura Lauth, Sydney Lea, David Lee and Jamila Trindle, Rodney Terich Leonard, Jen Levitt, Howard Levy, Owen Lewis, Matthew Lippman, Jennifer Litt, Karen Llagas, Sara London and Dean Albarelli, Clarissa Long, James Longenbach, Cynthia Lowen, Ralph and Mary Ann Lowen, Ricardo Maldonado, Myra Malkin, Jacquelyn Malone, Carrie Mar, Kathleen McCoy, Ellen McCulloch-Lovell, Lupe Mendez, David Miller, Josephine Miller, Nicki Moore, Guna Mundheim, Matthew Murphy and Maura Rockcastle, Michael and Nancy Murphy, Myra Natter, Jay Baron Nicorvo, Ashley Nissler, Kimberly Nunes, Rebecca and Daniel Okrent, Robert Oldshue and Nina Calabresi, Kathleen Ossip, Judith Pacht, Cathy McArthur Palermo, Marcia and Chris Pelletiere, Sam Perkins, Susan Peters and Morgan Driscoll, Patrick Phillips, Robert Pinsky, Megan Pinto, Connie Post, Kyle Potvin, Grace Prasad, Kevin Prufer, Alicia Jo Rabins, Anna Duke Reach, Victoria Redel, Martha Rhodes, Paula Rhodes, Louise Riemer, Sarah Santner, Amy Schiffman, Peter and Jill Schireson, Roni and Richard Schotter, James and Nancy Shalek, Soraya Shalforoosh, Peggy Shinner, Anita Soos,

Donna Spruijt-Metz, Ann F. Stanford, Arlene Stang, Page Hill Starzinger, Marina Stuart, Yerra Sugarman, Marjorie and Lew Tesser, Eleanor Thomas, Tom Thompson and Miranda Field, James Tjoa, Ellen Bryant Voigt, Connie Voisine, Moira Walsh, Ellen Dore Watson, Calvin Wei, John Wender, Eleanor Wilner, Mary Wolf, and Pamela and Kelly Yenser.